Guide to the passage tombs at

BRÚ NA BÓINNE

Newgrange, 3300 BC—
older than Giza Pyramids (2600 BC)
and Stonehenge (2200 BC).

View towards the passage from the end recess at Newgrange.

INTRODUCTION

Brú na Bóinne, where the great Stone Age tombs of Knowth, Newgrange and Dowth are situated, is a roughly U-shaped area, formed by a bend in the River Boyne. Here, on a shale ridge that rises above the low-lying countryside, in the centuries before and after 3000 BC people built the three majestic funeral monuments, as well as many other smaller tombs and related sites.

Brú na Bóinne's monuments are among the finest examples of stone-built tombs in Europe, with a very rich collection of megalithic art. They provide evidence for a remarkable concentration of ritual activities, involving the construction of monumental works that entailed a substantial investment in labour. As a result, for some centuries Brú na Bóinne was a place of action and activity.

The Bend of the Boyne was formed in ancient times when the river, just east of Slane, was blocked by a ridge of Carboniferous shale rock through which it could not flow. This forced it to make a right-hand turn to the south, where it

flowed east, parallel to the ridge, for about three miles. It then swung northward again, forming a loop. From here the river flows east and finally empties into the sea downstream from Drogheda.

The region formed by the Boyne and its northern tributaries extends for approximately five square kilometres. The land is low-lying and suitable for farming, covered by boulder clay deposited by Ice Age glaciers.

The people who built this huge cemetery were not the first settlers in Ireland, nor were they the first people to have lived in the fertile Boyne valley. Ireland itself had been settled from around 8000 BC in the Middle Stone Age or Mesolithic period. It is believed that these first settlers sailed here from northern and western Britain. They were hunter-gatherers, living off what the land and sea provided—wild animals, fish, berries and plants. The early people made simple tools from stone and bone, such as scrapers for preparing animal skins, stone blades and bone spears for fishing. Rivers were an important source of food. Forests too provided food and materials for early Neolithic people.

Farming had first developed in the Near East about 12,000 years ago, around the time when the Ice Age was coming to an end in Ireland. As a result, people gradually learned how to select and grow types of grasses and cereals, and to breed and keep pigs, oxen and goats, which gave them a stable food supply. With a reliable food supply throughout the year, agricultural communities developed and eventually replaced the older hunter-gatherer way of providing food. Society and economic activity became more complex and specialised. Long-distance trade in goods developed. This new way of life spread throughout western Asia and Europe, and eventually to Ireland. New methods and attitudes were introduced from abroad. As a result of the introduction of farming around 4000 BC, fundamental changes in everyday life took place. People no longer had to depend on what nature could provide but now cooperated with nature. Forest clearance commenced.

Around 3900 BC, at the beginning of the Late Stone Age (Neolithic), the first settlements appeared at Brú na Bóinne, and by 3500 BC considerable areas would have been open, farmed landscape.

As agriculture was adopted in Ireland, so too was the practice of building funeral monuments for the dead, using large stones. Such structures are called megalithic (*mega*, large; *lithos*, stone) tombs and were used for communal burial of cremated remains. Deposited with the remains were such personal items as beads and pendants made of bone, antler pins and, very occasionally, pottery.

Though Knowth, Newgrange and Dowth, stretching from west to east, dominate the landscape of Brú na Bóinne, they are just the core of a much larger cemetery, which holds 37 tombs and at least eight other individual sites of uncertain date. It is likely that additional sites have been destroyed over the millennia. As well as the three great mounds and their satellite tombs, there is a fourth cluster of tombs at Ballincrad townland between Newgrange and Dowth, two mounds lie south of the main cemetery on the floodplain of the river, and two sit to the north of the cemetery at Monknewtown and Townleyhall. There are also embanked circular enclosures of later date called 'henges', timber circles, a ceremonial procession route (cursus) and a ritual pond. There is evidence of other sites that have not yet been excavated.

A notable feature of the Newgrange mound is that it is oriented and built so as to allow the rays of the rising sun at the winter solstice, the days around 21 December, to enter the tomb and travel down the passage to shine directly onto the back chamber and flood it with dawn light. It is not known whether this was intended to be witnessed by anyone other than the remains of the dead, as the entrance to the tomb was closed by a large upright stone, nor do we know how the ancient people conducted their rituals inside and outside the tombs.

Building each of the three great tombs probably involved hundreds of people, working for many decades. It shows that a stable, organised community lived in the region, that they understood the movements of the sun, and that they could express their fundamental beliefs about death and the afterlife through elaborate architecture and symbolic art. They had the engineering skills to lift and move enormous stones over long distances, and the tools to cut wood, dig trenches, cut sods and carry out other construction work. They could organise large groups on complex projects over many years, and they could visualise the transforming effect of a beam of sunlight travelling along a dark passageway in a sealed tomb in the dead of winter.

The construction of the three great tombs at Brú na Bóinne shows a stable, organised community that understood the movements of the sun and expressed their beliefs about death and the afterlife through elaborate architecture and symbolic art.

Distribution map of passage tombs in the Boyne Valley.

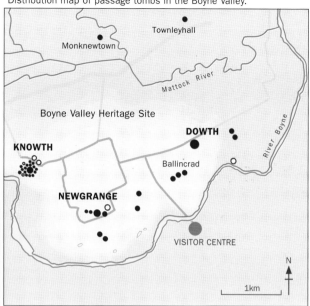

OWTH

EWGRANGE

OWTH

Boyne Valley Heritage Site

Top: Portion of western side of main mound and kerb, Knowth.

Centre: Newgrange from the south-west.

Below: Dowth from the east.

5

KNOWTH

NEWGRANGE

DOWTH

Left: View back along the passage of the western tomb at Knowth.

Centre: At the end of the passage, looking into the chamber area of Newgrange.

Right: Approaching the chamber from the passage in the northern tomb at Dowth.

PASSAGE TOMBS AT
BRÚ NA BÓINNE

There are four distinct clusters of tombs extending from west to east along the elevated ridge, and eight further individual sites. In all, there are 37 tombs, three of which are the commanding mounds of Knowth, Newgrange and Dowth. Another cluster of three mounds stands at Ballincrad, on lower ground between Newgrange and Dowth.

Knowth is the most westerly cluster of sites, followed west to east by Newgrange, Ballincrad and Dowth. There are further individual sites close to the River Mattock to the east, two to the north of the area, and three more in the low-lying Boyne floodplain south of the main ridge.

The Knowth main mound contains two passage tombs back to back, one facing eastwards and one facing westwards. The covering mound is delimited by 127 kerbstones. Nearby there are the remains of nineteen smaller tombs and a historical reference to a possible tomb across the road from the main mound.

Further east at Newgrange there are four tombs, with the great mound located on the highest point of the ridge. There are two smaller adjoining tombs, K and L, on the west side and a fourth (Z) on the eastern side with a fifth possible site (Z1) nearby. The size of the main mound can be gauged from the fact that it is 85m in diameter, and the internal passage alone is 19m long.

The entrance to the large Newgrange tomb faces south-east and the mound appears to have been built to incorporate the winter solstice on 21 December, just before the days start to get longer. Newgrange has a cross-shaped chamber with three end recesses where burials were placed in stone basins. In addition to these five tombs there are three more individual tombs in the Newgrange area (Sites A, B and U), one of which was enclosed in a henge (A).

At Ballincrad the remains of three mounds are set close together in a line. All have been badly damaged and the mounds reduced in height.

Dowth is the most easterly and least known of the great mounds. The tomb has two chambers with entrances on the western side and there are 115 surviving kerbstones. Inside the central chamber of the northerly tomb there is a stone basin and megalithic art, while the southern tomb is smaller. There are the remains of two passage tombs near Dowth and two possible others closer to Ballincrad, both damaged. There is a large mound, called Site B, in the floodplain close to the river.

Taking Brú na Bóinne as a whole, it is not certain whether there was a strategy for siting the tombs in relation to each other. The location of the three main tombs was determined by the builders' desire to use the highest ground within the cemetery. While the sequence of construction of the small tombs at Knowth has not been determined fully, their clustering indicates that there was an original tomb that acted as a focal point for successive tomb-building.

The linear arrangement at Newgrange, and possibly also at Ballincrad, may be the result of local topography. The other small tombs do not appear to have had a planned location in relation to each other and were probably built as the occasion arose.

Besides the large and smaller tombs, there are several other types of structure, which are of later date. These include a henge or circular embanked enclosure; a cursus or ceremonial procession route; stone circles; standing stones; an artificial ritual pond; and a pit and post circle. Not all of these have been excavated, but their purpose, whether ceremonial or functional, must have supported the central preoccupation of the site with the dead.

KNOWTH

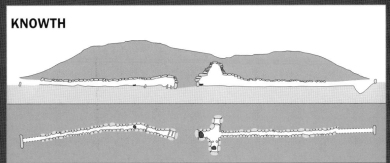

NEWGRANGE

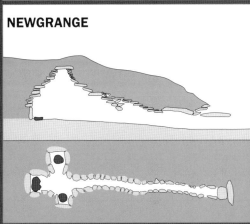

Plans and cross-sections of the tombs at Knowth, Newgrange and Dowth.

DOWTH

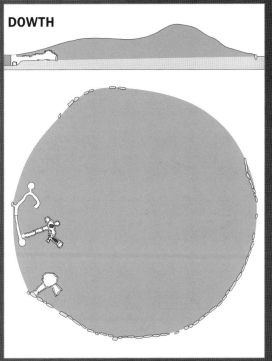

400 YEARS OF TOMB-BUILDING

Based on radiocarbon dating evidence, it seems that the tombs were built about the same time, approximately between 3300 BC and 2800 BC. It has not been established which tomb is the earliest. Most of the ^{14}C dating comes from cremated bone in the Knowth tombs, which would have been in existence before the burials were inserted.

There is evidence for extensions to the large mounds at Knowth, Newgrange and Dowth. At Dowth the north tomb started as a small structure that was enlarged. At Knowth the large mound was built in two stages, while at Newgrange's large mound there were three stages.

Sequential dating derived from the reuse of structural stones in the large tomb at Knowth shows that a substantial structure existed before even the earliest, inner part of the large mound was built. That also appears to be the case at the large Newgrange mound, where at least one stone from the previously mentioned tomb was used in the building of stage 1. The art on the destroyed tomb is very elegant and indicates the existence of developed art styles and possibly a developed society before the construction of the initial stages of both the large tombs at Knowth and Newgrange.

It may be the case, therefore, that at least one tomb pre-dates these sites, possibly by a couple of centuries back to 3500 BC, although use would have continued over the following six or seven centuries.

The notable point about Newgrange and Knowth is that radiocarbon dating shows that the tomb-building phase took place over a period of just 300 years, around 3300 BC, though the tombs would have been used for longer than that.

PASSAGE TOMBS

TYPES OF MEGALITHIC TOMBS

There are four types of megalithic tombs, which are named, according to their shape, 'court tomb', 'portal tomb', 'passage tomb' and 'wedge tomb'.

The building of great stone tombs in Ireland commenced at the beginning of the early Neolithic or New Stone Age, about 4000 BC, with court and portal tombs. The final type, the wedge tomb, was built a couple of thousand years later.

The only type of tomb found at Brú na Bóinne is the passage tomb, so called because inside the tomb a stone-built passage leads onto a chamber or a series of recesses at the back of the tomb.

The builders of passage tombs represented a separate tradition to those who built portal and court tombs. This tradition developed first along the western coastline of Europe, particularly the Iberian peninsula and Brittany, before spreading to Britain and Ireland.

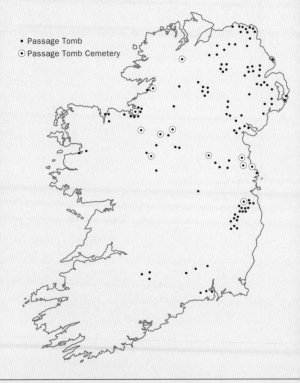

• Passage Tomb
⊙ Passage Tomb Cemetery

Distribution map of passage tombs in Ireland.

TYPES OF PASSAGE TOMBS

There are two main forms of passage tomb in Ireland. One is called 'undifferentiated' because the end of the passage merely widens out to form the chamber. The other type has a well-defined circular chamber out of which open three recesses, one at the end and one at each side. This design of passage tomb is called 'cruciform' or cross-shaped.

The passage and chamber sides were built by digging sockets or a trench into which the large upright stones or orthostats were set. Once in their sockets, the stones were reinforced by backfilled soil and smaller packing stones. In some tombs the passage and chamber were then covered by parallel lintels. The chamber roof was constructed in a technique called corballing. The roof was held in place by the weight of the mound above it. This was made up of alternate layers of sods, stones and clay. Many of the orthostats, capstones and some of the chamber roof stones were highly decorated. It is estimated that the Newgrange mound alone contained 200,000 tonnes of stone and could have taken 400 people 30 years to complete.

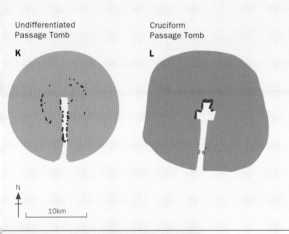

Undifferentiated Passage Tomb

Cruciform Passage Tomb

N

10km

Corballed roof at Newgrange.

Building a passage tomb was a huge undertaking. A society or community that built such a tomb would have to have been centrally organised. People would have needed to be living above subsistence level and to be able to accumulate a surplus of food in order to release workers to transport the materials and build the structures. A wide range of supporting resources would be needed: timber rollers to move the huge stones; tools to cut or quarry them; ropes to hold them; and boats or timber to float the stones from their source, which was often far away, to the building site. Because tombs were often built on a height, many large stones would have to be brought uphill.

In Europe, passage tombs are found only in two areas: the north, around the Baltic, and the west, on the continent's Atlantic coast, stretching from western Spain to the Shetland Islands. There are differences between the two European clusters of passage tombs, in ground-plan, grave-goods and burial rites. They have many features in common, however, such as the use of very large stones, the tendency to be built close to the sea, communal burial, the leaving of grave-goods and the use of art. They tended to be built in groups or cemeteries and to be located on high ground or mountain tops, sometimes in spectacular or eye-catching locations. There is no evidence for contact between the two groups, however.

In Ireland there are about 330 passage tombs, which are found mainly north of a line from Wicklow in the east to Sligo in the west. Certain distinctive features are found in all passage tombs. Inside the structure there is a passage and chamber made from large upright stones; these were covered by a circular mound or cairn built from smaller stones, earth or sods. The mound was bounded by a circle or kerb of large megaliths called kerbstones. From an opening at the edge of the cairn the passage leads into the chamber.

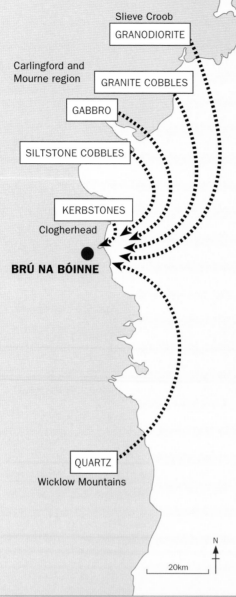

Slieve Croob
GRANODIORITE

Carlingford and
Mourne region
GRANITE COBBLES

GABBRO

SILTSTONE COBBLES

KERBSTONES
Clogherhead

●
BRÚ NA BÓINNE

QUARTZ
Wicklow Mountains

N

20km

Map of east coast of Ireland, showing possible source of stone and building materials for passage tombs at Brú na Bóinne.

BUILDING MATERIALS

In Brú na Bóinne the main structural stones are of greywacke, which is found in that portion of the Palaeozoic geological zone that stretches from the Irish Sea at Clogherhead to the north of Slane. Although it has not been established exactly where within this zone the stones come from, some aspects of their composition suggest that they were acquired at Clogherhead, north of Drogheda. If that was the source, the quarried stones would have had to be transported over a long distance, probably first by sea and then upriver to the Brú na Bóinne site. Once there, they would have had to be landed on the flat floodplain downstream from Newgrange. Two large standing stones at the edge of the ridge overlooking the river and floodplain may have marked the landing site.

Greywacke may have been used because it was less prone to weathering, and it would have been easy to apply the art to its smooth, flat surface. The greenish colour was probably another attraction.

Dolerite, sandstone and limestone were also used in the Boyne cemetery in smaller quantities, and they were sourced nearer to hand. A large pit south of the main site at Knowth may have been the source of some of the shale and some of the boulder clay and sods. Quartz used at Brú na Bóinne came from the Dublin/Wicklow mountains to the south, however, while the granite boulders and banded stones came from the Carlingford region to the north.

Quartz stone at Newgrange.

KNOWTH · **NEWGRANGE** · **DOWTH**

Left: Decorated basin stone in the chamber of the western tomb at Knowth, right-hand recess.

Centre: Decorated passage stone no. L19 at Newgrange.

Right: View along the passage toward the chamber of Dowth North.

RESTING PLACE, RITUAL AND SOLAR CYCLE

The structures at Brú na Bóinne are first and foremost an expression of the beliefs of the people who built them, in particular about death and the afterlife.

The passage tombs at Brú na Bóinne were preceded by a domestic settlement in the early Neolithic period, and were followed by the construction of other enclosures, over a period that stretched from 3900 BC to 2000 BC. Following the construction of the passage tombs, embanked enclosures or henges were built, associated with a type of pottery called Grooved Ware. Later again, further embanked enclosures were built, associated with another style of pottery called Beaker Ware.

The primary function of most of the tombs was to hold the remains of the dead. Excavations of nearly every tomb yielded bone and cremated remains.

The construction and orientation of the tombs show a knowledge of the sun's cycle, and possibly a need to mark the passage of the sun and the seasons. The Newgrange tomb was built so as to allow the rising sun to light up the back of the chamber in the days around the winter solstice (21 December).

The practice of building passage tombs on elevated sites or mountain summits may have been intended to ensure uninterrupted views of the skies, although the visibility of the tombs from a distance and creating a visible impact on the landscape seem to have been important considerations too. It is possible that the great sites at Brú na Bóinne may have been intended as a demonstration of the importance and power of their builders. Their development in size and complexity may have reflected a growing social stratification within the agricultural community, in which a group was able to organise and deploy the labour and resources of the entire population.

The decorated kerbstones around the great mounds, with their carved designs, may also have been focal points for procession. They suggest that the main public ceremonies took place outside the tombs, while only a few special people were allowed inside. There may have been processions around the mound, stopping at particular decorated stones. On both sides of the main Knowth mound, an inward curve of the kerb provides what could have been a gathering point. Most of these recessed areas of Newgrange and Knowth had a spread of exotic stones that

13

were sourced outside the locality. As the two Knowth tombs face east and west, it is possible that there were ceremonies there around the time of both the spring and autumn equinoxes, on 21 March and 21 September. This could have involved a day-long ceremony, starting at sunrise at the entrance to the eastern tomb and ending at sunset on the western side.

Henges, wooden circles and cursuses were designed for ceremonial gatherings. The earthen banks or timber circles that enclosed henges do not appear to have been a defence against outside agencies but rather were intended to enclose the activities taking place within; this type of monument has been described as 'an inward-looking amphitheatre'.

North-east of Dowth there is a very large, well-preserved henge overlooking the Boyne. Further north, near the River Mattock, is the Monknewtown henge. Excavation revealed twelve pits with cremated bone and a ring-ditch.

Two damaged henges, Site A and Site P, are located on the floodplain beside the river bank but are levelled and hardly visible.

Such henges were probably ceremonial centres. A different style of henge enclosure, one made of concentric circles of pits and post-holes that once held timber posts, lies just south-east of Newgrange mound. When in use, the 120m-wide enclosure probably looked like a ring of timber uprights. Many of the pits and post-holes contained cremated animal bone.

Also at Monknewtown is a man-made ritual pond, still containing water, which is enclosed by a 2m-high bank.

A cursus, which is a path or roadway through a landscape, appears to be designed so as to bring specific landscape features into view along the route, indicating the importance of ceremonial procession. East of the Newgrange tomb there is a possible cursus running north–south, with banks 20m apart.

Stone basin in the centre of Dowth North.

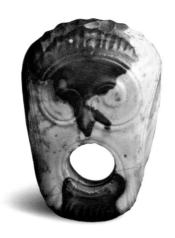

Above: Knowth at full moon, with reconstruction of late Neolithic timber structure outside the entrance to the eastern tomb.

Left: A phallus-shaped stone object found at the entrance to the western tomb at Knowth.

Below: Decorated flint mace-head found in the eastern tomb at Knowth.

15

THE BURIALS

When the Dublin merchant Charles Campbell and his workmen rediscovered the entrance to Newgrange in 1699 and entered the tomb, they reported seeing bones in the recesses, as well as 'barbarous sculptures'.

Burials in passage tombs take place mainly in the chamber and its recesses. The builders practised cremation, followed by communal burial. There is evidence that this usually took place on successive occasions. As a result, access to the chamber had to be maintained over time. They left personal items in the chamber with the cremated remains, mainly beads and pendants, probably portions of necklaces, mushroom-headed pins made of bone and antler, and small stone marbles. Small pieces of pottery have occasionally been found.

Most of the archaeological evidence shows the communal burial of many people, which was the practice in passage tombs. Not all of the people who built the tombs may have been buried there, however. The size and complexity of the tombs may indicate that the society of the tomb-builders was stratified, so it is possible that only members of an élite, perceived to have a special relationship with the dead or selected according to family lineage or special qualities, were interred there.

Professor M.J. O'Kelly's excavations at the large Newgrange tomb found little evidence for burial or grave-goods, but as that site had been open for centuries these could have been removed.

Some of the smaller Newgrange tombs also contained human remains. Tomb (Site) K yielded some cremated remains, along with chalk marbles, a hammer pendant, a bone pin and two flints. Tomb L contained cremated remains in different parts of the chamber, along with chalk marbles, bone pins and three pieces of pottery. Some disturbed cremated bone was found in tomb Z, and a stone basin on the eastern side of the chamber contained cremated bone, beads, marbles and a bone pin.

In the right-hand recess of Knowth's eastern tomb the remains of over 100 individuals were identified, over half of whom were juveniles. In some of Knowth's smaller satellite tombs the remains of only a few people were deposited.

The Dowth mound does not have smaller adjacent tombs. The mound was damaged over the years and an 1847 excavation revealed a stone basin in fragments and some human and animal bone.

The large, carved stone basins that are found on the chamber floor of each of the three Newgrange recesses, and at Knowth and Dowth, may originally have served as containers for the cremated remains. They are part of the original ceremonial layout of the tombs, and seven have been found to date at Brú na Bóinne.

Together with the existence of other communal structures, elaborate stone carvings on the kerbstones outside may indicate that public ceremonies took place outside the tombs. Possibly only a select few, perhaps community elders or religious leaders, were allowed to enter the sacred spaces within the chambers.

Owing to the practice of cremation, little evidence for features such as height and age is available; what exists suggests that people were of medium height and that their lifespan was short, less than 40 years.

There is little evidence of human activity at Brú na Bóinne in the Bronze Age and later Iron Age. When burials resumed, they were of a completely different type. Inhumation burials in the style of the Iron Age were made around the base of the Knowth mound up to the seventh century AD, but by then the builders of the great funeral monuments were long gone.

CORMAC MACAIRT

Cormac MacAirt was high king at Tara in the third century AD. The old Irish text *Senchus na Relec* ('The Lore of Cemeteries') says that he was one of three people in Ireland who believed in one God before St Patrick arrived. Traditionally, as high king, he would have been buried at Brú na Bóinne when he died, but Cormac didn't want to be buried in the old pagan cemetery and decreed that he be buried at Ros-na-Rig (Rosnaree, on the Boyne).

When Cormac died, his followers decided to bury him at Brú na Bóinne in the traditional way. When they reached the crossing-point at Rosnaree on the way from Tara, the river rose in flood three times and prevented the cortège from crossing over to Brú na Bóinne. Cormac got his wish and was buried instead at Rosnaree, outside the pagan burial place.

History and mythology are probably entwined in the figure of Cormac MacAirt. It is not known whether he was a historical figure who ruled at Tara and then became associated with mythological events and qualities that express universal themes of the hero figure and the wise king. He is regarded as the embodiment of the good king and is credited with having composed instructions, *Tecosc-na-Rig*, on how a wise king should act to ensure the good of the tribe. These were written down in the ninth century. He is said to have reigned in the period AD 227–267.

Above left: Basin stones in the right-hand recess at Newgrange.

Below left: Decorated stone, orthostat 49, in Knowth West resembling a stylised human being.

Below right: View of the eastern side of the main mound at Knowth, tomb 14 in foreground, tomb 13 in background.

Legend says the mound at Newgrange was dedicated to the Dagda, the sun god of pre-Christian Ireland.

The light of the winter solstice shines along the passage at Newgrange.

SOLAR ALIGNMENTS

The orientation and design of many passage tombs show that the builders were greatly interested in the cycle of the sun's movements across the sky and through the seasons. At Newgrange, Knowth and elsewhere in Brú na Bóinne that interest is reflected on a spectacular scale. This suggests that the sun's cycle must have been part of the beliefs or world-view of the tomb-builders.

There would have been practical reasons for this interest also. The sun's cycle turns the seasons and hence the cycle of food production. The practice of agriculture, and therefore the survival of the community, depends on direct knowledge of the sun's movements to a far greater degree than do hunter-gatherer societies. Such life-giving solar movements may have been acknowledged and celebrated.

Reliance on the movement of the sun and stars is also strong among seafarers who wish to navigate over long distances. There is no evidence of a continued interest in long sea journeys among the Neolithic farming communities in the millennia after the earliest settlers arrived. It is thought, however, that the tomb-builders of Brú na Bóinne were influenced by ideas that originated in western Iberia. Similar types of passage tombs, megalithic art and grave-goods have been found in the Orkney Islands, Wales and Brittany. Such a shared artistic repertoire indicates knowledge of the sea, navigation and boat-building.

While many tombs at Brú na Bóinne seem intended purely for the interment of the dead, solar events—particularly at the solstices and equinoxes, the key turning points of the year— may have been a factor in their orientation. At the spring and autumn equinoxes, 21 March and 21 September, night and day are of equal length. The longest day occurs at the summer solstice, 21 June, while the longest night occurs at the winter solstice on 21 December. After that date the days start to lengthen and the sun's warmth starts gradually to increase.

The two entrances to the great mound of Knowth face approximately east and west, probably to mark some aspect of the rising and setting sun, perhaps at specific times of the year, such as the equinoxes. This interest in the sun's movements may also have been linked to the fortunes or afterlife of the dead within the tomb. At Dowth, the entrances to the two chambers are on the western side.

Newgrange represents its builders' interest in the sun's cycle in the most dramatic fashion. The entire structure as it was finally designed admits the light of the sun rising in the south-east at a precise time of the year, 21 December, showing that it had a specific function of marking the winter solstice. Had the builders not been so ingenious, the size of the internal passage and the natural slope of the land would actually have prevented this from happening. Because the tomb is so large, the passage is especially long, at 19m, and it slopes downward towards the entrance because of the natural slope of the ridge on which it sits. The builders, however, designed the roofbox to overcome these obstacles.

The roofbox is an opening directly above the main tomb entrance; two large upright stones form a gap between the top of the first roofstone and the bottom of the second. Through this opening, rather than through the main entrance,

NEWGRANGE SUNRISE

Another tradition, but a more modern one or at least one more familiar in modern times, had been mentioned to us by many visitors particularly in the early stages of the excavations when we were working almost totally in the dark as far as factual information was concerned. This was to the effect that a belief existed in the neighbourhood that the rising sun, at some unspecified time, used to light up the three-spiral stone in the end recess. No one could be found who had witnessed this but it continued to be mentioned and we assumed that some confusion existed between Newgrange and the midsummer phenomenon at Stonehenge. Since Newgrange faces south-east it was clear that no such comparison was valid but when we began to think about it, we realized that it might be worthwhile to investigate the winter solstice when the sun rises in that quarter. We first did so in 1967. On 21 December 1969 we recorded the following observations on tape:

At exactly 8.54 hours GMT the top edge of the ball of the sun appeared above the local horizon and at 8.58 hours, the first pencil of direct sunlight shone through the roof-box and along the passage to reach across the tomb chamber floor as far as the front edge of the basin stone in the end recess. As the thin line of light widened to a 17cm band and swung across the chamber floor, the tomb was dramatically illuminated and various details of the side and end recesses could be clearly seen in the light reflected from the floor. At 9.09 hours, the 17cm band of light began to narrow again and at exactly 9.15 hours, the direct beam was cut off from the tomb. For seventeen minutes, therefore, at sunrise on the shortest day of the year, direct sunlight can enter Newgrange, not through the doorway but through the especially contrived slit which lies under the roof-box at the outer end of the passage roof.

[M.J. O'Kelly, *Newgrange: archaeology, art and legend* (London, 1982), 123–4.]

the solstice sunlight streams at dawn to move steadily along the sloping passage and light up the back recess of the burial chamber.

Some structural alterations took place during conservation work in the area of the roofbox, and it is not known whether these affected the entrance of the sunlight. It appears, however, that the relevant stones were replaced as close as possible to their original location. At present the sun shines into the chamber at the solstice, but that achievement is part of a complicated story owing to the fact that the tomb was not built as a single piece of work but in three stages. One has to assume that the tomb in its first stage was designed to allow the sun to penetrate the chamber. To maintain that arrangement, great care had to be taken with the design of the next stage, and even greater care during the third and final stage. The integration of all three stages so as to admit the sun's rays was an enormous achievement.

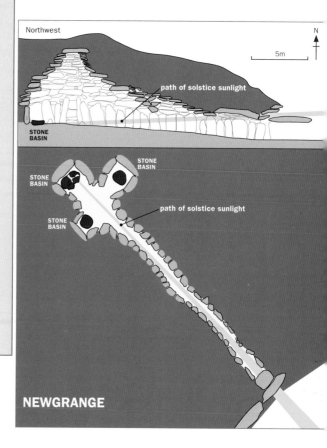

NEWGRANGE

Decorated kerbstone no. 15 at Knowth with complex combinations of motifs.

MEGALITHIC ART

Within the two Atlantic passage tomb regions, two types of art are found: art applied to small grave-goods such as pottery, and artwork applied to the structural stones of the passage tomb itself, which is called megalithic art. The latter is an exclusive feature of passage tombs along Europe's Atlantic coast and does not occur in the Baltic area.

Megalithic art is particularly abundant at Brú na Bóinne. There are over 280 decorated stones within the large tomb at Knowth alone, 110 at Newgrange and about 40 at Dowth. At Knowth a further 25 stones that may have been part of other, damaged tombs are also to be found, and at least 50 more are to be found at the smaller tombs. Knowth alone has as many decorated stones as all the known decorated stones from passage tombs abroad. The total number for Brú na Bóinne is likely to have been much greater as not all sites have been excavated and others have been destroyed.

Although it is mainly abstract, the megalithic art in Brú na Bóinne almost certainly expresses in symbolic form its creators' beliefs about life, death and the ordering of the universe, in a language we cannot read or understand.

The motifs found in Irish megalithic art are either angular, such as lozenges, triangles and zigzags, or curved, such as concentric circles, spirals and ovals. Such artwork was applied to the surface of large structural stones, mainly

21

the orthostats, capstones and kerbstones. The cupmark, which is a picked hollow shape, is a very ancient motif in rock art. Nearly half of the Newgrange kerbstones show the cupmark, though it appears much less inside the tomb.

Megalithic art at Brú na Bóinne shows different styles, blending a distinctive Irish style with Breton and Iberian influences. Different styles and motifs can be found at the different tombs; for example, the use of spirals and lozenges is more associated with Newgrange, and the carving that resembles a face on orthostat L19 within the Newgrange passage has parallels in southern Spain and Portugal. On the other hand, the linear style of stone ornamentation found on some of the Knowth stones is similar to that of Brittany.

Both motifs and methods evolved over time. Even the artwork on particular stones was not completed at one time but shows signs of having been added to later, with further motifs superimposed on earlier patterns.

The stones were carved using four techiques, the most common of which were incision and picking. With incision, an edged implement such as a piece of flint or quartz is dragged along the stone surface to make a line, usually a straight

line or an angular pattern. With the picking technique, punch-like tools with rounded points of varying size were the main implement. A stone was used to hammer the punch to create a series of close-set impressions on the rock surface. This technique could produce a variety of shapes, curved as well as angular. A slight modification of this method was the 'picked linear' or 'false relief' technique, where a series of deeper and wider lines were cut into the surface, creating a prominent pattern. This technique, along with incised motifs, is largely found at Brú na Bóinne. Another variation was 'area picking', which was used to form motifs such as a lozenge. A more common method was 'dispersed picking', sometimes called 'pick dressing', in which punch impressions on the surface could be either dispersed or set close together.

A final technique is referred to as sculpture because it involved shaping an object from a natural block of stone. The large stone basins from Brú na Bóinne are examples of this technique. After the basins were shaped, artwork was applied to some.

Some motifs may be slightly representational or functional. The motif on orthostat 49 in the

Above left: Detail of carvings on kerbstone at Knowth.

Below left: Carvings on Dowth kerbstone no. 51.

Illustration right: Decorated kerbstone on north side of Newgrange.

Detail of Newgrange kerbstone no. 52.

western tomb of the large mound at Knowth vaguely resembles a stylised human being, probably wearing a loose-fitting garment. On a kerbstone at Knowth's large tomb there is a panel of four carved stones of which the central two have circular motifs resembling eyes that look towards Newgrange kerbstone no. 52.

Within the eastern tomb of the large mound at Knowth, angular motifs are found at high and low levels, the latter on the orthostats. Within the earliest stage of this eastern tomb, such art is found on the outermost capstone and on the inner capstone, where the art forms a conjoined motif on the base of the two capstones. At floor level, at each end of the passage, there is a sill stone. In both the main Newgrange mound and Knowth's eastern chamber there is angular art on opposite corbels directly above the end of the passage.

Overlaid motifs show that art was applied at different times. Incised angular motifs are the earliest, followed by picked angular, then dispersed area picking. Broad lines or ribbon art then becomes common and, finally, close area picking.

The highly decorated stones around many tombs had a ceremonial function. Although originally the carved motifs may have complemented rituals carried on inside the tombs, there is evidence that gradually the emphasis shifted to the outside and that the external art became increasingly prominent. The decorated kerbstones around the Newgrange, Dowth and Knowth tombs may have become the focus of public ceremonies that the whole community could participate in or witness, possibly in the form of processions around the mounds with certain stones acting as focal points.

Detail of decorated basin stone in right-hand recess of Eastern tomb at Knowth.

FORGOTTEN CEMETERY REDISCOVERED

Brú na Bóinne appears to have been either forgotten or neglected during the Bronze Age and the early Iron Age, in the first and second millennia BC. Excavations showed no evidence of the use of the tombs or their immediate area in that period. Over the next 2,000 years the area was ritually and culturally dormant, though it may have functioned as farming land.

Revival occurred at the end of the first millennium BC and the beginning of the first millennium AD. This was ritual in nature and consisted at Knowth of a small cemetery of graves that contained inhumation burials with grave-goods such as necklaces of glass beads, while at Newgrange an area was set aside where various artefacts were deposited. The presence of objects such as bronze brooches indicates limited human activity about the middle of the first millennium AD, but it was later, about the eighth century, that major changes took place. Around AD 800 Knowth became the royal residence of the kings of northern Brega, now the equivalent of present-day Meath and south Louth. These were part of the rising Uí Néill dynasty. For the next 300 years or so, this ruling family dominated politics in eastern Ireland, and the Knowth settlement became like a small village between the ninth and eleventh centuries.

The inhabitants lived in rectangular wooden houses, a number of which were associated with underground storage and protective chambers called souterrains. This was a self-contained settlement of people who practised mixed farming and who were served by skilled craftsmen in bone, metal and stone. During the tenth century the Knowth settlement reached its pinnacle. Its king, Congalach Mac Máel Mithig, also known as Congalach Cnobga, who died in AD 965, became high king of Ireland. Around that time, as a result of settlement expansion, some of the small passage tombs were badly damaged and a number of their large structural stones were used in the construction of souterrains.

There is no evidence for anything similar at Newgrange, but a souterrain was built at Dowth possibly about the same time, which suggests that it too may have been a dwelling place.

Brú na Bóinne is mentioned in twelfth-century Irish records such as the Book of the Dun Cow and the Book of Leinster, but the information about the monuments and their setting in the landscape refers to earlier times.

In the mid-twelfth century Tigernan Ua Ruairc, the king of Breifne, controlled Brú na Bóinne for a period. Later in the same century the Anglo-Normans occupied the top of the large mound at Knowth for a time. In 1142 most of the Brega lands were given by Tigernan Ua Ruairc to the recently arrived Cistercian monks of Mellifont, who established monastic farms or granges at Knowth, Newgrange and other places in the locality. From this Newgrange got its name.

During the Middle Ages the area remained prosperous; the western portion, Knowth, remained part of the lands of Mellifont, while the eastern portion passed to the Anglo-Norman family of the Nettervilles. A tower-house and a church were constructed at Dowth. A church and cemetery were also established in Monknewtown.

As a result of the Reformation, the lands of Knowth were confiscated from the Cistercians. Most of the land passed to a new Protestant class, some of whom remained in the area until fairly recent centuries.

The significance of Brú na Bóinne began to be rediscovered about 300 years ago, though initially

DISCOVERY OF KNOWTH

Professor George Eogan's account of the discovery of the western passage at Knowth on 11 July 1967.

At last I was convinced that the entrance had been found: we set out on our hands and knees to investigate. It proved to be a thrilling, if rather worrying, experience. At 10m from the entrance we had to crawl under an orthostat that had partly fallen inward. Next it was necessary to wriggle through a pool of muddy water on the floor beneath a couple of leaning orthostats. Loose stones on the floor made our crawling rather uncomfortable, and it grew difficult to judge how far we had come, yet there was no sign of an end to the passage.

Eventually the roof began to rise in height and we could almost stand upright. Nearly all the orthostats appeared to be decorated, and the whole structure was more impressive. At one point a stone basin lay in the passage. Then, coming to a sill, we illuminated the orthostat on its inner right side and beheld what seemed to be an anthropomorphic figure with two large, staring eyes. This ghostly guardian suggested that we were approaching the inner sanctum. But we still had several metres to go, now walking erect and easily except for some boulders on the floor. The end of the passage was finally reached: an undifferentiated chamber with two sillstones. The outer sill and the rear stone of the chamber were decorated, apart from the vertical line, in a manner similar to that of the kerbstone before the entrance—with concentric rectangles.

We remained speechless for some time and marvelled at the achievement of these anonymous passage tomb builders. Here was truly one of their great enterprises of close to 5,000 years ago . . .

What a day!

[G. Eogan, *Knowth and the passage tombs of Ireland* (London, 1986), 32–3.]

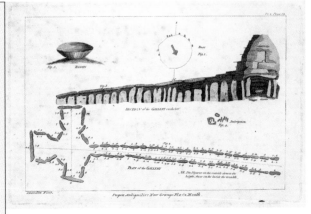

Above: Plan and cross-section of the great tumulus at Newgrange, with detail of the chamber-plan, decoration and a stone basin. Published *c.* 1791–4.

Below: Earliest plan of Newgrange: Lhwyd's survey of Newgrange, 1699.

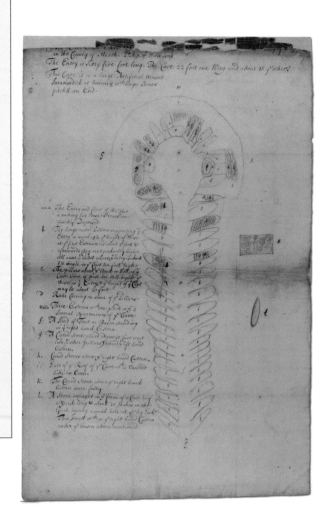

not in a benign way. In 1699 a Dublin merchant, Charles Campbell, who had acquired the Newgrange lands, set about removing some of the large stones from the mound for road-making. Workmen discovered carving on a large stone at the base of the mound. Campbell and his workers then discovered an opening behind the stone and, on entering the mound, found a chamber 20ft high where, in the recesses, they found 'barbarous sculptures' and some bones. The early antiquarian Edward Lhwyd, Keeper of the Ashmolean Museum in Oxford, was in the area and heard about the removal of the stones. He noted the entrance leading to the chamber and made a plan and description of the find, writing to tell Dr Tancred Robinson of the Royal Society, London, of the discovery on 15 December 1699.

The Newgrange site was described again, this time by Thomas Pownall, a former governor of Massachusetts, in February 1773 in the British journal *Archaeologia*. This included plans and sections of the tombs. He also noted the presence of another tomb site. A number of other antiquarians visited Newgrange over the following centuries but did not leave any detailed information about the site or its context.

About 1770 the Dowth landowner, Viscount Netterville, built a summer-house or a tea house on the Dowth summit, but there is no evidence that he discovered its interior chambers. In 1769 Thomas Pownall had noted a feature at Dowth that he called a 'cove', possibly a chamber or a recess of a tomb. In 1775, however, the artist Gabriel Beranger described the site as a 'sepulchre' mound that had not yet been opened. In 1834 the antiquarian George Petrie referred to a chamber built from large stones. In 1847 the Royal Irish Academy excavated part of the Dowth mound; this work did not reveal anything but left a crater on the summit. In a

Watercolour of Newgrange in 1775 by Gabriel Beranger.

work published in 1848 W.K. Wakeman referred to the presence of two tombs. After it came into state ownership in 1881, conservation work at Dowth by the newly appointed Inspector of Ancient Monuments, Thomas N. Deane, revealed the souterrain. In 1932 the then Inspector of National Monuments, Harold G. Leask, carried out some investigation and found some of the kerbstones on the western and eastern sides.

Scholarly studies started to appear in the nineteenth century. In 1836 the first Ordnance Survey published the first detailed map of the area at a scale of six inches to the mile. One of the Ordnance Survey scholars, John O'Donovan, recorded the place-names and some landscape details of County Meath, including those around Brú na Bóinne.

Some time before 1870 a local tenant, Mr Tiernan, built a wall above the kerb at Newgrange, which acted as a facing for the cairn, and he also dug a trench outside the kerb.

In 1881 the British Parliament passed an Ancient Monuments Act, which brought the three great mounds into state care. The appointment around the same time of the first Inspector of Ancient Monuments, Sir Thomas Deane, resulted in some protective measures at Newgrange.

In 1892 a major study on the megalithic art of Brú na Bóinne, especially that of Dowth and Newgrange, was published by George Coffey.

Small excavations took place in the early twentieth century, including the uncovering of some of the Dowth kerbstones by Harold Leask. In 1941 R.A.S. Macalister excavated a small tomb at Knowth and exposed the outer part of 58 kerbstones of the large mound.

A programme of modern investigation and conservation began in the 1960s. Professor George Eogan excavated a passage tomb that overlay a habitation site at Townleyhall. In 1962 research and excavation, which continue today, began at Knowth. In the same year, Professor M.J. O'Kelly started excavating Newgrange and continued until 1975. A large programme of conservation accompanied these excavations, including the construction of a vertical wall nearly 3m high by using stones that lay on the ground surface on the outside of the kerb. These stones are irregular in shape and if used in the wall they would have backed onto the mound, which would not have provided a stable backing as it was largely formed from loose stones.

In view of such conditions, it would have been impossible to ensure that such a wall would stand. That which exists today is supported by a reinforced concrete wall. It is unlikely, therefore, that such a feature existed originally; more probably the exotic stones from which the present wall is built formed part of a spread that was laid down on the old ground surface outside the entrance of the tomb on the completion of mound-building. This seems to have been the case at the western and eastern tombs of the large mound at Knowth. Some other investigations also took place, such as those carried out by David Sweetman at enclosures at Monknewtown and Newgrange.

Newgrange passage tomb in 1908.

MAESHOWE

NEWGRANGE

Left: Thought to date from around 2700 BC, Maeshowe is the largest and most impressive of Orkney's chambered cairns.

Right: Winter solstice at Newgrange.

SHARED TRAITS OF ATLANTIC COASTLINE

The passage tombs on the Atlantic coastline differ from the northern European tombs in ground-plan, burial rites and the nature of grave-goods. Nevertheless, they share several common features. The tombs, built from large stones, are located fairly close to the sea; they contained communal burials, and grave-goods were left with the dead.

Art in the northern European tombs appears as geometric motifs applied to pottery. In western and southern Iberian tombs it was applied also to objects such as stone plaques and what have been described as 'idols'.

The Atlantic passage tombs probably originated in the southern and western portions of the Iberian peninsula or Brittany. Tombs there have a number of features in common, such as tomb form and structure, artefacts, art and location. Often the tombs were located on elevated ground, as is the case at Brú na Bóinne.

Cultural influences from these different regions appear at various sites within Brú na Bóinne. At Knowth the undifferentiated passage tomb, akin to earlier 'prototypes' in Atlantic Europe, is the most common ground-plan. Elsewhere in Ireland the cruciform layout is more common, but at Brú na Bóinne the two types were used simultaneously.

It is in the area of megalithic art that Brú na Bóinne is most aligned with, and simultaneously most different from, other Atlantic zone tombs. Such art, usually non-representational motifs incised on large structural stones, is found from southern Iberia to the north of Scotland.

Angular motifs are found on some structural stones and on grave-goods within the tombs in Iberia, whereas curvilinear art is more common in Brittany. One of the most dramatic carved stones, which marks the approach to the western

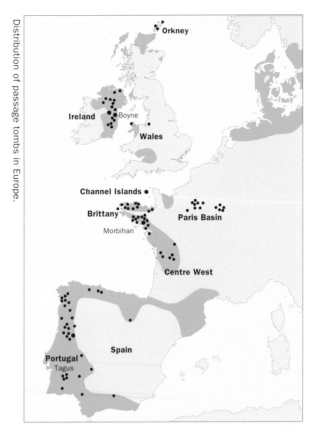

Distribution of passage tombs in Europe.

chamber at Knowth (orthostat 49), resembles a human face with huge staring eyes and is very similar to megalithic art in Brittany. A similar 'face' carving (orthostat L19) at Newgrange finds parallels in carvings from southern Spain and Portugal.

The Boyne artists sometimes developed motifs found elsewhere; for example, a form of linear design from Brittany is developed into large-scale areas of picking at Knowth and Newgrange.

Over the tomb-building period an indigenous style developed at Brú na Bóinne, including a flowing, ribbon-like form of decoration, and later motifs were often added alongside older patterns. The quintessential Irish megalithic motif, the spiral, is only common in Ireland and is typical of the earlier art style, whereas lozenges in false relief represent the more developed style. The spiral motif is also found on other tombs, for example at Slieve na Calliagh, but it is very rare outside Ireland. Later, megalithic designs appeared that seem to have been inspired by the overall shape of the stones.

Three specific carving techniques are largely confined to Brú na Bóinne: picked linear, in which deep, wide lines create designs that stand up from the surface of the stone, often called 'false relief'; incision, where an edged piece of stone is drawn along the surface, forming angular or straight patterns; and area picking, or dressing.

Left: Tustrup-dysserne, the largest passage grave in Eastern Jutland, Denmark, dating from *c*. 3200 BC.

Below: The quintessential spiral motif at Newgrange.

Brú na Bóinne and the passage tomb achievement

Over time, the Brú na Bóinne passage tombs became one of Europe's most important cemeteries. As well as being an area of outstanding architectural and artistic significance, Brú na Bóinne probably influenced other areas, not only in the Boyne valley but also up the Blackwater valley, notably at Slieve na Calliagh (Loughcrew) and Oldcastle. Its influence may have extended even further, being perhaps reflected in the construction of the west Wicklow group of tombs and the tombs inland from Carlingford Lough in north Louth, south Armagh and Down.

Brú na Bóinne's influence can be found elsewhere in Ireland. One such site is Knockroe, south Co. Kilkenny, but some of the Sligo tombs were probably also inspired by the Boyne region. Inspiration was not confined only to Ireland. Tombs in Anglesea in north Wales, and in the Mersey region not far away, have similarities with Brú na Bóinne, as do tombs much further away, especially in the Orkney Islands off northern Scotland.

All this evidence demonstrates the key role played by Brú na Bóinne during the course of the Neolithic era about 5,000 years ago.

Glossary of terms

CAPSTONE
The final stone placed on a corbelled roof to seal the roof gap, or a stone placed on top of a stone tomb or monument.

CARBON DATING
A method of dating organic material by measuring the extent of decay of the carbon-14 radio-isotope within it, because carbon-14 decays at a fixed, known rate.

CARROWKEEL WARE
A decorated form of pottery vessel that appeared around the third century BC and is frequently associated with passage tomb burial. The decoration was applied by pressing a pointed or rounded object into the wet clay to make a pattern over the surface.

CORBELLED ROOF
Rising or domed roof formed by laying large stones on top of each other, each overlapping the one below on the inner side, thereby bringing the roof gap gradually inward to the point where it can be covered and completed by a single slab.

CURSUS
A man-made area in the landscape formed by two parallel ditches or banks, often ending in a U-shape or right angle. They are believed to have been ceremonial or processional routes.

FLINT
A form of hard chalk, which could be shaped and polished to form sharp pointed and edged tools during the Stone Age.

GREYWACKE
Sandstone with a grey-green tinge.

GROOVED WARE
A type of pottery that appeared towards the end of the Late Stone Age. It had straight or slightly curved sides and was decorated with straight, even lines or grooves.

HENGE
A circular space used for ritual, communal ceremony and possibly astronomical purposes, created by building an enclosing structure of earth or timber.

INHUMATION
Burial by placing the body in the ground.

LOZENGE
Diamond-shaped pattern.

ORTHOSTAT
Large upright stones that line the passage and chamber of a tomb.

PALAEOZOIC
Geological period that began approximately 600 million years ago, often applied to rocks of that era.

POST-HOLE
The remains of a hole that was dug to hold a timber post, to act either as a freestanding structure or as a supporting upright for another structure. The remains of post-holes are often recognised by a circle of different-coloured soil and they can indicate where a structure once stood.

RING-DITCH
Bronze Age and Iron Age circular burial monument, which has a flat central area enclosed by a circular ditch or bank.

SCRAPER
Stone tool, usually of flint, used to scrape hides clean or to work timber.

SILL STONE
A horizontally placed floor stone that separates or defines different sections within the tomb, e.g. separating the passage area from the recess.

SOUTERRAIN
An underground, stone-built passage, sometimes forming a tunnel and/or chambers, in which food was stored or people could take refuge. They date from the early medieval period, c. fifth–twelfth century AD.

31

Further reading about Brú na Bóinne

Brennan, M. 1983
The stars and the stones.
Thames and Hudson, London.

Coffey, G. 1912
Newgrange and other incised tumuli in Ireland.
Hodges Figgis, Dublin.

Eogan, G. 1986
Knowth and the passage tombs of Ireland.
Thames and Hudson, London.

Herity, M. 1974
Irish passage graves.
Irish University Press, Dublin.

Jones, C. 2007
Temples of stone.
The Collins Press, Cork.

Mitchell, F. and Ryan, M. 1997
Reading the Irish landscape.
Town House, Dublin.

O'Brien, T. 1988
Winter solstice at Newgrange.
Ríocht na Midhe **8**, 50–9.

O'Kelly, C. 1973
Passage grave art in the Boyne Valley.
Proceedings of the Prehistoric Society **39**, 354–82.

O'Kelly, M.J. 1982
Newgrange: archaeology, art and legend.
Thames and Hudson, London.

Ó Ríordáin, S.P. 1979
Antiquities of the Irish countryside (5th edn).
Methuen, London.

O'Sullivan, M. 1993
Megalithic art in Ireland.
Town House, Dublin.

O'Sullivan, M. 2005
Duma na nGiall. The Mound of the Hostages, Tara.
Wordwell, Bray.

Prendergast, K. 2004
Caves of the winter sun.
Ríocht na Midhe **15**, 12–25.

Shee Twohig, E. 1981
The megalithic art of western Europe.
Clarendon Press, Oxford.

Shee Twohig, E. 1990
Irish megalithic tombs.
Shire Publications, Princes Risborough.

Smyth, J. 2009
Brú na Bóinne, World Heritage Site, Europe.
The Heritage Council, Kilkenny.

Stout, G. 2002
Newgrange and the Bend of the Boyne.
Cork University Press, Cork.

Wilde, W. 1849
The beauties of the Boyne and Blackwater.
James McGlasham, Dublin.

Image credits

Cover and back: *Ken Williams.*
Page 1: Megalithic art. *Photographic Unit, DEHLG.*
Page 2: Newgrange. *Photographic Unit, DEHLG.*
Page 5: Knowth. Newgrange. Dowth. *Ken Williams.* Map of Ireland. Map of passage tombs. Cartography *Matthew Stout.*
Page 6: Knowth. Dowth. Newgrange. *Ken Williams.*
Page 7: Plans and cross-sections of the tombs at Knowth, Dowth and Newgrange. Cartography *Matthew Stout.*
Page 8: Drawing of kerbstone (*after Coffey 1912*) *Royal Irish Academy.*
Page 9: Jamb stone at Knowth. *Ken Williams.*
Page 10: Knowth. *Ken Williams.* Distribution map of passage tombs. Cartography *Matthew Stout.*
Page 11: Plans of passage tombs. Cartography *Matthew Stout.* Corballed roof, Newgrange. *Photographic Unit, DEHLG.*
Page 12: Map showing possible source of materials. Cartography *Matthew Stout.* Inside tomb. *Ken Williams.*
Page 13: Knowth. Newgrange. Dowth. *Ken Williams.*
Page 14: Stone basin, Dowth. *Ken Williams.*
Page 15: Knowth at full moon. *Ken Williams.* Phallus-shaped stone. *National Museum of Ireland.*
Page 17: Basin stones, Newgrange. Decorated stone, Knowth. Mound, Knowth. *Ken Williams.*
Page 18: Newgrange. *Ken Williams.*
Page 20: Plan and cross-section of solstice sunlight at Newgrange. Cartography *Matthew Stout.*
Page 21: Knowth. *Ken Williams.*
Page 22: Newgrange. *Ken Williams.*
Page 23: Kerbstone, Newgrange. Kerbstone, Knowth. Passage stone, Newgrange. *Ken Williams.* Illustration of kerbstone, Newgrange (*after Coffey 1912*) *Royal Irish Academy.*
Page 24: Knowth. *Ken Williams.*
Page 26: Tumulus at Newgrange. *Courtesy of the National Library of Ireland.* Lhwyd's survey of Newgrange. *The Board of Trinity College Dublin.*
Page 27: Watercolour of Newgrange. *Royal Irish Academy.*
Page 28: Newgrange 1908. *DEHLG.*
Page 29: Maeshowe. *Charles Tait Photographic Limited.* Newgrange. *Ken Williams.*
Page 30: Distribution of passage tombs in Europe. Cartography *Matthew Stout.* Tustrup-dysserne. *Charles Tait Photographic Limited.* Spiral motif at Newgrange. *Photographic Unit, DEHLG.*